SELFIE
WITH CHERRY

POEMS BY
BETH COPELAND

GLASS LYRE PRESS

Copyright © 2022 Beth Copeland
Paperback ISBN: 978-1-941783-90-0

All rights reserved: Except for the purpose of quoting brief passages for review, no part of this book may be reproduced or transmitted in any form or by any means, electronic or mechanical, including photocopying, recording, or by any information storage and retrieval system, without permission in writing from the publisher.

Design & Layout: Steven Asmussen
Cover Art: LaWanda Walters

Glass Lyre Press, LLC
P.O. Box 2693
Glenview, IL 60025
www.GlassLyrePress.com

Selfie With Cherry

CONTENTS

Half Moon	1
Second Wife	2
Obsession	3
Don't Think it Couldn't Happen to You	4
Abandoned Nest	5
Pyre	6
Familiar	7
Deconstructing "Orange," My First Love Poem For You	8
Divorce	10
My 40-Year-Old Daughter Says I'm Boy Crazy	11
I Snap a Selfie with a Cherry	12
The O of Letting Go	13
Erasing a Poem I Wrote for You	15
Men with Dead and Dying Wives Want Me	18
One Nightstand	19
Aubade	20
Lady Bug, Lady Bug, Fly Away Home	21
Ephemeroptera	22
Giving up the Ghost	24
Text with an Ex	25
Outer Banks	26
Single, Blue	28
My Daughter Paints a Mountain	29
If Love Comes	31
Selfie on My 69th Birthday	32
Acknowledgments	35
About the Author	37

Half Moon

Tonight's moon reminds me
of a black-and-white photograph

Gabriel took many years ago. One
side of my face flooded

with light, whiter than a geisha's
talc-painted cheek, the left

dark as if a line's
drawn down the middle; one eye

swims in phosphorescence
while the other

stares into starless
night. Maybe

Gabriel loved me
but couldn't

say it, taking pictures
instead, studying curves

of a face he would carve
into a linden mask. I haven't

thought of Gabriel in years. Did he
go back to Lebanon after the war?

Is he in heaven with the angel
he was named for? I wish

I could hear his side of this
story, but I have only mine—half

shadow, half shine

Second Wife

Fifteen years ago I drove south to see you as trees broke
into bloom—redbuds, pears, dogwoods—and my heart
unfolded like a bud closed too long in the cold.

Later, I moved into the log cabin built when you were
still married to a woman with chestnut hair that spilled
around her shoulders as she knelt in the dirt as if in

prayer, planting dozens of bulbs on the edge of woods.
Sometimes I wished we didn't live where her daffodils
burst yellow and green—worthy of Wordsworth's ode—

along a ditch beside the gravel road, a reminder of the life
you'd shared with her. I wished I'd never seen the wooden
box with recipes written in her hand on faded index cards—

Tomato and Basil Rigatoni, Amish Bread, Blueberry Cobbler—
and the wedding photographs stashed face-down in the drawer
of a bedside chest. I wished you'd never told me about the rugs

she wove on a loom in our bedroom. I wished she hadn't left
that green, down-filled vest from L.L. Bean in the hall closet.
It's not my style, I said when you offered it to me. *It looks*

like a life jacket. As I slipped it on, I hoped it wouldn't fit.
I was tired of living in a house with your ex-wife's ghost.
So sick of it! As I zipped it up, you said, *It's perfect.*

Obsession

A string of obsidian beads
counted one by one. I speak your name
as an incantation, replaying scenes—that night
at the Rolling Stones concert in the rain, soaked
to the bone and happy. What happened?
When did it change? Obsession's the corkscrew
to the heart in Bob Dylan's song. A poison.
A perfume. One, two, three. Obsession,
remembering moments I can't change.
A wine glass shattering on the kitchen tile.
Falling down drunk on the firewood, I lie
on my back in the snow, wanting to die.

If I left an angel behind, it was without wings
spread, writhing, wrestling with demons.
Months later, you asked if you were the dark
angel in the song I posted on Facebook. No,
you were the man who yanked me to my feet,
leaving fingermark bruises on arms you said
were so spindly you could snap them like twigs.
Who are you? you shouted, so angry spit sprayed
from your mouth onto my face. *Who are you?*
I'm the raven at your window in *Love Minus Zero/
No Limit.* The wound compressed into coal.
The black diamond on another woman's hand.

Don't Think it Couldn't Happen to You

You could end up in a motel with a neon *NO
VACANCY* sign in the window or in a cheap
studio apartment sleeping on a blow-up bed.

Don't think of it as failure. Instead,
think of it as rebirth like a phoenix rises
from flames or a snake leaves its skin behind.

Maybe your flesh is too tight now that you've grown
or maybe you needed to burn down to nothing
but feathers and bones before you could fly.

Abandoned Nest

You show me a nest, a bowl of pine straw, moss,
and leaves with three eggs like speckled jelly beans,
hardened, unhatched; we wonder what happened,

why the bird left, and laugh about weird locations
where wrens build nests—on a grapevine wreath,
in the crotch of your jeans on the clothesline.

Later, I look at properties on my laptop, dreaming
of a place of my own, a condo in long-leaf pines
or a brick church I could convert into a home.

I pack miniature houses in bubblewrap to ship to
my daughter and sift through a battered footlocker
of old diaries and letters too heavy to lift, deciding

what to keep, discarding the rest. When did we quit
trying? When did the life we warmed with our breath
turn cold? When was our ending etched in stone?

Pyre

When I return to the cabin, Kasey runs to greet me.
Separated for nine months—long enough to bring new life
into the world—I pet his head but don't hug you. *I don't want you*

to move to the mountains, you say. *Let's take a walk.* But halfway
to the road, I notice dead branches on the dogwoods and stop
to snap them. You break the bigger boughs until there's a gap

through the thicket. Then we move to the pines, breaking brittle
limbs with dry, brown needles, our hands sticky with sap. Our dog
is bored with us and retreats to the porch while we labor until it's too

hot to continue. *Enough wood for a bonfire,* I say, recalling the night
we torched a dead Christmas tree, drinking white wine and dancing
around the leaping blaze and the dark morning I burned your love

letters in a metal trash can outside, drunk and weeping, *liar! liar!
liar!* as your false words folded into flames. You laugh, crack the last
branch from the trunk, and say, *You always loved playing with fire.*

Familiar

Grief is a big black dog that leaps on you when you don't see it coming. You think it's outside, but here it is, in the house with you, a stray that keeps coming back in different forms. It's the death of someone you love, the end of a marriage, the loss of a career, an opportunity that will never return. It's an addiction you've had your whole life but always denied. It's a betrayal of trust, a ruptured rapture. You offer the dog water and food. It's always here, why not feed it? You pet its silky head and gaze into its dark eyes. It becomes your best friend, your companion for life.

Deconstructing "Orange," My First Love Poem For You

I wrote it in couplets because I wanted to be coupled
with you. I wasn't thinking of the uncoupling to come.

>*Unrhymed, orange stands alone like a man without
>the chime of a woman's voice in his house.*

I was thinking of you in the log cabin I hadn't visited yet.
The subtext of all your email messages was loneliness.

>*It's the color of sunlight and blood seen through closed eyelids,
>of marigolds, Mexican sunflowers, and Monarch butterflies.*

Funny that I mentioned closed eyes! I couldn't see
what lay ahead. All that flowery stuff is fluff.

>*of Dreamsicle clouds drifting across the skyline at dusk,
>of tangerines, tiger lilies, trumpet vines, and rust.*

How romantic I was! At least, until the last word—*rust*.
Perhaps a premonition that our love would self-destruct?

>*It's the glowing globe that opens
>in his hand, lobe by lobe,*

I pictured you peeling an orange. Were the lobes the halves
of the brain I didn't use when I fell in love with you?

>*identical, but not quite, like the slant rhyme
>of Southern light on tamarind and pine.*

I liked the *rind* in tamarind, how it tied in with the fruit.
The *pine* was you pining for an ex-girlfriend who'd dumped you.

>*It's the citrus scent of gin and Seville bitters
>as he peels the rind, as each segment splits on its seam*

After we split up, I considered myself the bitter—not better—half.
Isn't it codependent for couples to be halves of the same whole?

> *without tearing, as he pares the white Valencian lace*
> *of the inner skin from a crescent of fire*

Sometimes an orange, like a cigar, is just an orange, but in this case,
I was so besotted with you that it became a striptease on the page.

> *and tastes the summer heat, the heart's desire.*
> *If only you were there to share its sweetness …*

That summer was hot in more ways than one. Sizzling, humid.
Humiliated, I was angry you still wrote letters to a woman you'd lost.

> *He would give you the moon and the stars if you asked.*
> *He divides the sun. He offers you half.*

I never asked for more than half, and you rarely gave it.
No one owns the sun. It was never yours to split.

Divorce

A tree with twin trunks entwined
reminds me of us wanting to grow

old together, skin to skin, bole to bole,
heart to heart, halves of the same whole.

Known as *gemels*—from the Latin word
meaning "a pair"—did their trunks fuse

into one, or did one sapling split in two
like twin flames sprung from one soul?

Tomorrow I'll sign the papers, but today
I study the branches, how they overlap

and bend, sharing shade and light. Where
does one tree start and the other one end?

My 40-Year-Old Daughter
Says I'm Boy Crazy

Even when the boy is 70-plus, I get a stupid
schoolgirl crush. I send her photos of men I like
and she checks them out on eHarmony and Match.
That one looks nice, she says. Maybe too nice.

I don't want a choir boy. I like the bad ones, dark
with five o'clock shadows and deeply furrowed brows.
Retired versions of James Dean, rebels, rabble-rousers.
Artists, musicians, poets. Men who will break my heart.

Don't trust that one, she says. But he's the one I want.
The mystery man, felt fedora aslant, flexes his biceps
in a bathroom mirror. *You know what's under that fedora,*
she says. *A big old bald head.* So, what? Bald is beautiful.

A guy on Plenty of Fish who calls himself White Wolf—
with snowy hair down his back and a Hulk Hogan mustache—
wears tight leather jeans and likes to party. *If you don't drink,
there are plenty of other ways to get lit,* he writes, *wink, wink.*

BigBob69 is seeking "nothing serious" and wants to sweep
me away on his Harley. Could I squeeze into my skinny jeans
and purple cowgirl boots, balance on the back of his bike,
wrap my arms around his waist, and trust him with my life?

Damian from Damascus sports a sleeve of tats—tidal waves,
tribal bands, a blue sunburst—and plays the slide guitar.
I bet he's smokin' hot on the stage! *Mom, are you crazy?*
Maybe, maybe not. Who says I have to act my age?

I Snap a Selfie with a Cherry

between my teeth, its stem still attached.
You like that it matches my lipstick,
my bold, bad girl smile. I'm not

your wife though I grieve with you as she sleeps
in the rented hospital bed in your guest room.
She's leaving you, forgetting how

to speak, hold a spoon, sit up without
help, and you wonder when she'll forget
how to swallow, how to breathe.

I greet you before sunrise and after sunset
on my side of the continent, texting over currents
of light and sound waves on a computer screen.

I've been thinking of you all day. I scroll
through photographs on Facebook—you in a kayak,
lifting the oar over your head in triumph, jubilant

to be on the water and free from caregiving
duties for the afternoon. When I say your dark
eyes could melt through my flesh like fire

through snow, you respond with a blue heart emoji.
I scroll down to an oval photograph of your wife
as she once was—her eyes shining, her face

framed with ash blond hair. I want to taste the sun
that slants into your eyes as you drive, the rain
on your lips. Alone, I bite into the sweet

flesh, spit out the stone, and swallow the rest.

The O of Letting Go

The perimeter of your circle is zero,
a zone I was never supposed

to enter, the emptiness
left in the gold O

removed from your finger
with the words *Divine Appointment*

engraved inside the ring. I comfort you
in stolen moments as you grieve

for the one slowly leaving, her lips
open in a soft O as she breathes

in and out like the ocean
in the poem you wrote for her.

You wrote a preamble for me
about a forbidden fantasy,

a rosy aureola you touched
in your imagination, only

you didn't use the languid
rolling O of *aureola*. No,

your word was *nipple*, stiffened
with that short i and the tip

of a fictive finger. You say Sade's
"The Sweetest Taboo" reminds you

of me. *I like it when you say O, O,
O, you say. It gets me so

turned on.* Still, you long with the longest
O for your beloved's return, while I,

the unloved one, moan and mourn
for you, for what you're losing,

for what we've lost, the lowing O's
of longing and love that won't

let us go.

Erasing a Poem I Wrote for You

Part One: Erasing Myself

In your preamble,

you stomp   your boots

Snow glistens in your beard, eyelashes, hair.

                    yes

                    light glows

                              on   white
sheets

like honey

Part Two: Erasing You

Snow
                          I know there's no

no   only the *yes* of

       winter's

                                  white
sheets

                    and

                 blood
      roses

Part Three: Erasing Us

                                    nothing

                                        no

          spark

                                    the white

        petal opens   into

                  breath

Men with Dead and Dying Wives Want Me

to comfort them. To be a temporary stand-in. The first man's wife has Alzheimer's. He's like her father and she's his child, an oversized baby in pull-up briefs. We talk online, and I say what he wants to hear— that he has a big cock, that I want him to fuck me, that he can come in my mouth. I get up every morning in the dark so I can talk to him before he leaves for work, coming back every night to stroke his flagging ego. He sends dick pics and says I'm sexy for a woman in her 60s. He's fond of me, he says, but no, he doesn't love me. Falling in love with her was like seeing Nirvana. She's the only woman he ever trusted. He doesn't trust me. He says I'll find someone else.

Eventually, I do. The other man's wife is dead. Her clothes hang like ghosts in the closet, some she never wore, still with tags. He hasn't thrown out her mirror, mascara, or hairbrush yet, but he likes the little black dress I wear to the poetry reading, my black stockings and boots, my silver and onyx necklace. He sits in my kitchen and stares at me with his dark Svengali eyes. *Would you like some dessert?* I ask. *Yes,* he says. *I want you.* I hold out as long as I can, telling him I'm not ready for a relationship yet, but one night I invite him into my bed. Have I died and gone to heaven? Later, he asks why, if I wasn't ready, did I change my mind. *Because I wanted to feel alive.*

One Nightstand

Painted mystic green, with bronze handles shaped like twigs
and knobs like sycamore leaves, with three drawers to store

lingerie, lavender oil, and a flashlight, it's a solo piece.
The first man I've slept with since leaving my husband

lies on the side where I usually sleep. I face a window
darkened with heavy velvet drapes I haven't replaced

since moving to this house in the mountains months ago.
Those red curtains make my bedroom look like a bordello!

Later, I lie there listening to him breathe. In the morning,
we turn to each other again. But is it love we're making?

Our bodies bud and blossom in the light, but does love
hover above the headboard like a hopeful sprite, or is it

wishful thinking? He makes a quick getaway with a zip
lock bag of bran muffins I baked the day before. Sure,

I could buy another nightstand where he can keep
his glasses, phone, and keys. I could become a two

nightstand woman, but is he a one-night stand man?

Aubade

An old French form, a love-lorn
serenade. At dawn I bade you

farewell at the door, slipping
my tongue in your mouth

as if I could inscribe my name
on the tip of yours. *Aubade*.

How passionately we obeyed
our bodies' biddings until

it was time for you to leave my sweet
abode. If I could bring you back

by plying our trade, playing with words
the way you would, I would. If I could

feel your tongue stir beside mine
again, as we shared one last kiss

for the road—*ah, babe*—I'd hold on
longer, knowing the end I now

know. You loaded bags in the trunk,
boots, a box of books, pages

and pages of poems written
in a diner that serves breakfast

all day. *Aubade*. A ballad sung as we
part and depart for parts unknown.

I lie on the unmade bed we made
love on and read your poems aloud,

each word cold in my mouth
like a polished stone.

Lady Bug, Lady Bug, Fly Away Home

He arrives in October at the peak of the plague.
Clinging to windows, walls, and desk, they fall
onto the floor and bed, scarlet carapaces
like Egyptian scarabs or scabs. Sweeping them
onto a piece of paper, he discards them at the base
of a burning sumac, but they return in droves,
orbiting his head as he writes in the night.

After he leaves, I dust, sweep, mop, burn
incense and sage, but insects don't respect
the boundaries of water and smoke. Wintering
in the cabin, they bleed yellow when I budge them
with a broom to check if they're sleeping or dead.
Seven spots for Our Lady's seven joys and sorrows,
for the seven nights he spent in my bed.

A lady bug hitched a ride home with me, he writes
from Ohio. *Girl cooties,* I reply. *I like your cooties,*
he says, but he's never coming back. Maybe that hitch
hiker laid eggs in his house. Maybe when leaves turn
to fire in the fall, hundreds of blood-colored bugs
will hatch on his walls. Maybe he'll gently nudge
one onto a page of his poetry and think of me.

Ephemeroptera

Like mayflies with lives so brief
there's time only for mating

in flight, maybe our pairing
was too fragile to be exposed

> *At dawn or dusk, they rise*

to light without being
destroyed. He left for dead

lines and debt, the demands
of step-children, rain-ruined

> *from water, where they waited as*

roof, books and bookings,
while in my Ephemera Museum

a diorama of insects
with delicate, diaphanous

> *nymphs for years. Males dance,*

wings hover above a wrinkled
lake. I toss his crossed-off

to-do list into the trash
with other scraps

> *lifting wings into ultraviolet light.*

never intended to last, an envelope flap
with penciled phone number

and the restaurant receipt
from dinner the night we got lost

                                        Scattered on the wind, mayflies

on a rutted road with barns, cows,
and fences on the left and falling

rocks on the right. He asked if we should turn
around, but—always hopeful—I said *Let's*

                                                     mate in the air.

keep going, until we hit the flooded
road ahead and he had to back up

slowly for half a mile or more
and return to the start. Later,

                                        One couple remains conjoined

he placed his hand on his heart
as if pledging allegiance

to whomever he wanted me to be—
a mythical woman, a muse,

                                           and flutters to the ground.

but once the deed was done,
he was gone.

Giving up the Ghost

Striking a match to a bundle of dried sage, I watch
smoke spiral to the ceiling like a departing ghost.

I wave a wild turkey feather around these rooms,
spreading fragrant fumes into closets and corners,

summoning guardian angels to remove his breath,
the press of his mouth on mine, his onion-husk voice.

Why did you ghost me? I texted after he left.
I didn't, he replied. *If I had, I wouldn't answer.*

Later, when I learned about the woman he returned to
and another one he bedded a week before visiting me,

I blocked him on Facebook, my email, and phone.
I want to forget the stars on the night we drove home,

how we stood in the halo of blue halogen headlights
at the door. *You're right,* I type in a text I'll never send.

I ghosted you.

Text with an Ex

Me: My latest dating site suitor is an Elvis impersonator. I. Give. Up.

Ex: I can do Elvis if that's what you want.

Me: Thank you. Thank you very much.

Ex: I'm just a hunk o' hunk o' burning love.

Me: How well I know …

Outer Banks

Your mouth tastes of mint, cigarettes, and salt.
Here, on the edge of the continent, we walk

as waves drive us up the dunes and Cleo,
your blue heeler pup, herds us back together.

Your salt-and-pepper hair curls at the collar,
wild in the wind. You slicked it down in the mirror,

but nature has its own mind. I like the gray stubble
on your chin, your Cool Water and cannabis cologne.

At the tidemark, I search for shells, calico scallops
and clams without jagged edges or cracks,

while you hand me broken pieces worn smooth
by waves, lustrous fragments that look like jade,

a white petal with a purple stripe. *Maybe I could bore
a hole in it and wear it on a cord around my neck*, I say.

You hand me more and more and more until my pockets
overflow. Rubbing a smooth gray shard, I worry

that we don't have enough in common, that you smoke
too much, that I don't always understand or like your jokes,

that sometimes you hug me so hard my ribs hurt,
pinning me to the hotel bed as if I might float away

without the weight of your body to anchor me,
that you keep an unopened bottle of booze

in your house to prove to yourself that you won't
drink it, that you got the DT's when you quit,

that your heart was so enlarged you almost
died but you don't think you're an alcoholic,

that you say you love me after knowing me only
two weeks, that I'll drown in these rough currents.

Cleo lassoes your feet, leaping to lick your hand as I lag
behind, still seeking that one perfect shell in the sand.

Single, Blue

A butterfly lands on the gravel road,
and I recall the first time we met for coffee

at Bohemia and the stranger who told us about a flurry
of blue butterflies in a tree after his mother died.

We talked about India and your Sanskrit tattoo.
I liked the cotton scarf cocooned around your neck.

We met for coffee, lunch, coffee, lunch—but never
touched. You'd disappear for weeks—even

months—and just when I thought you were gone
for good, you'd emerge from a chrysalis of silence.

I stop to catch my breath and watch the butterfly open
and close its wings as if signaling in code. *Yes, no, yes, no.*

With wings closed, it almost vanishes like a leaf
in the road; wings spread, it glows

with iridescent blues and black mantilla lace.
Is it a message from my mother? Is she speaking

from the other side? I don't know, but I know
what she'd say about us: *Don't wait*

for a man to decide if he wants you or not.
Fly solo. I'm letting you go.

My Daughter Paints a Mountain

She wasn't thinking as her brush swept
across canvas in wave-length strokes,

channeling a crest she'd never seen,
while I was still in the Sandhills

where there aren't any hills, just fields
of cotton, soybeans, and cedar stumps

in swamp water, sleeping on an air mattress
in a small apartment with prints and paintings

propped against walls instead of hung,
newly separated, newly sober, living

between the husband and home I'd left
and a haven I hadn't found yet.

*****

As I drove up a steep road to see a house
in the Blue Ridge, a large buck leapt

in front of the car to welcome me,
and I knew I'd found my new home.

I didn't know the mountain seen at the top
of the hill was the mountain she'd painted

months before, and she didn't know I'd move
to that house with a view of the mountain

she'd painted as if in a dream or fugue.
How could her mountain—purple, lavender,

pink, and forest green swirled to a peak
with white streak of snow against a blue sky—

mirror the one framed in my window?
Was it coincidence or synchronicity

that the mountain in her mind's
eye was more map than metaphor?

It was a message from the universe:
You're home. Open the door.

If Love Comes

It will come when I'm walking down the hill, listening
to songbirds and wishing I knew their names.

It will come with a mountain stream that wends
through culverts beside the gravel road.

It will come when I'm picking golden ragwort,
white trillium, and purple larkspur,

when I'm waking to the mountain's sleeping
face, to rabbits and deer, to the greening

trees, to gray fog and mist, to woodsmoke,
snow, stars, and sun, to burning

leaves of sumac and maple, to wild
violets blooming between stones.

It will walk with me, pouring sweet
water from a deep well, blue

fire, and a drumroll of thunder
when it comes.

Selfie on My 69th Birthday

This heart-shaped face with broken
capillaries tells a story of bearing

witness and giving birth, of being
firmly rooted to earth. Each line

is a statement of survival,
each wrinkle, a word on the wind;

these age spots, a route of the sun's
slanted rays, each silver hair—I refuse

to call them gray—a testament
to time, a reflection

of moonlight on water, of smoke
and storms, of a woman becoming

invisible and being
reborn.

Acknowledgments

Acknowledgment is made with gratitude to the following publications for poems that originally appeared in them:

Carolina Woman: Selfie on my 69th Birthday

Claw & Blossom: Pyre

Disquiet Arts: Aubade; Outer Banks

Abrazos: Dove Tales 10th Anniversary Anthology: Letters from the Self to the World: Don't Think It Couldn't Happen to You; Obsession; Erasing a Poem I Wrote for You

Epoch: Divorce

Goddess Anthology (The National Beat Poetry Foundation, Inc.): Selfie on my 69th Birthday

Hole in the Head Review: Single, Blue

Live Encounters: Abandoned Nest

Naugatuck River Review: Half Moon; Second Wife

The New Southern Fugitives: Lady Bug, Lady Bug, Fly Away Home

Peauxdunque Review: I Snap a Selfie with a Cherry; Men with Dead and Dying Wives Want Me; The O of Letting Go

Smoky Blue Literary and Arts Magazine: My 40-Year-Old Daughter Says I'm Boy Crazy

About the Author

Beth Copeland is the author of *Blue Honey,* 2017 Dogfish Head Poetry Prize winner; *Transcendental Telemarketer* (BlazeVOX, 2012); and *Traveling through Glass*, 1999 Bright Hill Press Poetry Book Award winner. She owns and operates Tiny Cabin, Big Ideas™, a retreat for writers in the Blue Ridge Mountains.

exceptional works to replenish the spirit

Glass Lyre Press is an independent literary publisher interested in technically accomplished, stylistically distinct, and original work. Glass Lyre seeks diverse writers that possess a dynamic aesthetic and an ability to emotionally and intellectually engage a wide audience of readers.

Glass Lyre's vision is to connect the world through language and art. We hope to expand the scope of poetry and short fiction for the general reader through exceptionally well-written books, which evoke emotion, provide insight, and resonate with the human spirit.

Poetry Collections
Poetry Chapbooks
Select Short & Flash Fiction
Anthologies

www.GlassLyrePress.com

www.ingramcontent.com/pod-product-compliance
Lightning Source LLC
Chambersburg PA
CBHW030202100526
44592CB00009B/411